IoT in Agriculture

Enhancing Crop Management and Sustainability with IoT Solutions

CW01425783

Carl Keyness

IoT in Agriculture
© Copyright 2023 by Carl Keyness
All rights reserved

TABLE OF CONTENTS

CHAPTER 1: INTRODUCTION TO IoT IN AGRICULTURE

The Role of IoT in Modern Agriculture

In recent years, the world has witnessed a technological revolution that has significantly impacted various industries, and agriculture is no exception. The integration of the Internet of Things (IoT) into agriculture has brought about a transformation that is often referred to as Smart Agriculture or Precision Farming. This chapter explores the pivotal role of IoT in modern agriculture and its implications for the farming industry.

Agriculture has been a fundamental part of human civilization for thousands of years. From the earliest days of crop cultivation and animal husbandry, farming has been essential for providing sustenance and driving economic growth. However, traditional farming practices have faced numerous challenges, including resource inefficiency, climate variability, and the need to feed a growing global population.

The advent of IoT technology has introduced a new era in agriculture, offering innovative solutions to age-old problems. IoT, in essence, involves the interconnection of everyday objects to the internet, enabling them to collect, exchange, and analyze data. In agriculture, this means that various devices and sensors can be deployed across farmlands to monitor and manage crucial aspects of farming, such as soil conditions, weather, crop health, and livestock management.

One of the key strengths of IoT in agriculture is its ability to gather real-time data from various sources and make it accessible to farmers and agricultural professionals. This data can be harnessed to make informed decisions that improve efficiency, increase productivity, and reduce resource wastage. For instance, IoT can provide farmers with data on soil moisture levels, enabling them to optimize irrigation, thus conserving water and reducing costs.

Moreover, IoT offers the potential for automation and remote monitoring. Tractors and other farm machinery equipped with IoT sensors can operate autonomously or be remotely controlled, reducing the need for manual labor. This is particularly advantageous as the agricultural labor force in many regions is dwindling, and there is a growing demand for increased agricultural productivity.

The significance of IoT in modern agriculture goes beyond mere convenience and efficiency. It addresses several pressing global challenges, including food security and environmental sustainability. With the world's population expected to reach 9.7 billion by 2050, agriculture needs to produce more food with fewer resources. IoT plays a vital role in achieving this goal through precision farming.

Precision Farming and Its Significance

Precision farming, often used interchangeably with precision agriculture, is a farming management concept that leverages IoT technologies to optimize various agricultural practices. The core idea is to customize farming operations to suit the specific needs of individual fields, crops, or even individual plants and animals. This precision leads to improved resource utilization, reduced environmental impact, and enhanced profitability.

The significance of precision farming can be understood through its various components and the benefits it offers:

Data-Driven Decision Making: IoT sensors and devices continuously collect data on soil conditions, weather, crop health, and livestock behavior. This data is then processed and analyzed to provide actionable insights for farmers. For example, if a sensor detects that a certain area of a field is experiencing nutrient deficiencies, a farmer can precisely apply fertilizers only where needed, reducing waste and increasing crop yield.

Efficient Resource Management: IoT technology enables precise control of resources such as water, fertilizer, and pesticides. By optimizing the use of these resources, farmers can significantly reduce costs and minimize the environmental impact of agriculture. Water scarcity is a global concern, and precise irrigation management can help conserve this precious resource.

Crop Monitoring and Disease Management: IoT sensors can monitor crop health, detecting early signs of disease or stress. Farmers can take timely action, such as targeted pesticide application or adjusting irrigation, to prevent widespread crop damage. This not only safeguards crop yields but also reduces the need for chemical inputs.

Livestock Management: Precision farming extends to animal husbandry, allowing farmers to monitor the health and behavior of livestock. Wearable devices and sensors can track vital signs and location, enabling early detection of illness and optimizing feeding schedules.

Sustainability and Environmental Benefits: Precision farming practices, guided by IoT data, can help reduce the environmental impact of agriculture. Efficient resource management, reduced chemical usage, and the preservation of natural ecosystems contribute to a more sustainable and eco-friendly approach to farming.

Increased Productivity and Profitability: By optimizing operations, reducing waste, and ensuring healthier crops and livestock, precision farming ultimately leads to increased productivity and profitability for farmers. This is especially crucial in a world where the demand for agricultural products is ever-growing.

Connectivity and Remote Monitoring: IoT in precision farming enables remote monitoring and control. Farmers can access real-time data and make adjustments to farming operations from anywhere with an internet connection. This level of flexibility and control is particularly valuable in today's fast-paced world.

IoT has emerged as a transformative force in modern agriculture, offering solutions to some of the sector's most pressing challenges. Precision farming, powered by IoT technology, plays a pivotal role in ensuring sustainable, efficient, and productive agricultural practices. The ability to collect and analyze data from various sources and apply it for data-driven decision-making is revolutionizing the way farmers approach their work.

CHAPTER 2: SMART SENSORS AND DATA COLLECTION

The Importance of Agricultural Sensors

In the realm of modern agriculture, the role of sensors cannot be overstated. These small but crucial devices are the linchpin of the Internet of Things (IoT) in agriculture, facilitating the collection of real-time data that is instrumental in decision-making, precision farming, and overall farm management. This chapter delves into the importance of agricultural sensors, the various types employed in IoT applications, and the critical aspects of data collection and management in the agricultural context.

Agricultural sensors are the eyes and ears of smart farming. They provide the means to gather detailed information about the environment, crops, and livestock. These sensors are designed to capture data on a wide range of variables, including but not limited to soil conditions, weather patterns, crop health, water levels, and animal behavior. The data collected by these sensors is transmitted to a central system for analysis and interpretation, allowing farmers to make informed decisions.

The importance of agricultural sensors lies in their ability to transform farming from a traditional, resource-intensive practice into a precise and data-driven operation. Here are some key reasons why these sensors are indispensable in modern agriculture:

Data-Driven Decision-Making: Agricultural sensors enable farmers to collect real-time data on various aspects of their operations. This data forms the foundation for informed decision-making, allowing farmers to take timely and precise actions based on accurate information. For instance, soil moisture sensors can help optimize irrigation schedules, ensuring water is used efficiently and crops are not overwatered.

Increased Productivity: By monitoring crop health, livestock conditions, and environmental factors, sensors help farmers identify issues or opportunities for improvement. This proactive approach can lead to increased productivity, better crop yields, and healthier livestock.

Resource Efficiency: Sensors play a crucial role in resource management. They can monitor the usage of water, fertilizers, and pesticides, and farmers can adjust application rates based on real-time data. This leads to more efficient resource utilization, cost reduction, and a reduced environmental impact.

Early Detection of Issues: Sensors can detect early signs of problems, such as crop diseases or pest infestations. Farmers can intervene promptly, preventing extensive damage and the need for large-scale chemical treatments.

Remote Monitoring: Many agricultural sensors offer remote monitoring capabilities, enabling farmers to keep an eye on their farms even when they are not physically present. This level of connectivity and accessibility is invaluable in modern farming.

Types of IoT Sensors in Agriculture

Agricultural sensors come in various forms and serve different purposes. They are designed to capture data from different aspects of farming, providing a comprehensive view of the agricultural environment.

Here are some of the key types of IoT sensors commonly used in agriculture:

Soil Sensors: Soil sensors measure parameters such as soil moisture, temperature, pH levels, and nutrient content. These sensors help farmers understand the condition of their soil, enabling them to make precise decisions regarding irrigation and fertilization.

Weather Sensors: Weather sensors gather data on atmospheric conditions, including temperature, humidity, wind speed, and precipitation. This data is crucial for managing weather-related risks and optimizing planting and harvesting schedules.

Crop Health Sensors: Crop health sensors monitor factors like chlorophyll levels, leaf temperature, and canopy size. They provide insights into the overall health of crops, enabling early detection of stress or diseases.

Water Quality Sensors: These sensors assess the quality of water sources used for irrigation and livestock. They can detect contaminants and ensure that water is safe for agricultural use.

Livestock Monitoring Sensors: Wearable devices equipped with sensors can track the health, location, and behavior of livestock. These sensors help farmers identify signs of illness and optimize feeding schedules.

Remote Surveillance Cameras: While not sensors in the traditional sense, cameras are often integrated into agricultural IoT systems. They provide visual data, allowing farmers to monitor the condition of crops and livestock, detect intruders, and track equipment and vehicles.

Environmental Sensors: These sensors capture data on broader environmental factors, including air quality, carbon dioxide levels, and radiation. They are valuable for assessing the impact of farming on the surrounding ecosystem.

Data Collection and Management

Data collection and management are integral components of any IoT system in agriculture. The data collected by agricultural sensors is a valuable resource, but it must be processed, analyzed, and translated into actionable insights. Effective data management ensures that farmers can make informed decisions and maximize the benefits of precision farming.

Data collection in agriculture involves the continuous gathering of information from sensors deployed throughout the farm. These sensors transmit data through wireless networks to a central hub or cloud-based platform. The data collected typically includes measurements and readings related to soil conditions, weather, crop health, and livestock well-being. The frequency of data collection can vary, with some sensors providing real-time updates and others transmitting data at regular intervals.

The management of agricultural data encompasses several critical processes:

Data Storage: The first step in data management is storing the collected information. The data may be stored locally on a farm's server or in the cloud. Cloud-based storage is becoming increasingly popular as it offers scalability, accessibility, and data security.

Data Processing: Raw data from sensors may require preprocessing to remove noise and outliers. Data processing algorithms can clean the data and ensure its accuracy. Data aggregation may also be necessary to combine data from various sensors for a comprehensive view of the farm.

Data Analysis: The next phase involves analyzing the data to extract meaningful insights. Data analysis techniques, including statistical analysis, machine learning, and data visualization, can uncover trends, anomalies, and correlations within the data.

Decision Support: The results of data analysis provide valuable information that can guide decision-making. Farmers can use these insights to adjust farming practices, such as altering irrigation schedules, applying specific treatments to crops, or taking action to improve livestock health.

Reporting and Visualization: Data management systems often include reporting and visualization tools that present data in a user-friendly format. Visual representations, such as charts and graphs, help farmers understand and interpret the data more effectively.

Alerts and Notifications: Many IoT systems are equipped with alerting mechanisms. When certain conditions or thresholds are met, such as extreme weather events or critical changes in sensor readings, the system can send alerts or notifications to farmers or farm managers.

Data Security: Protecting agricultural data is essential, as it often contains sensitive information about farm operations. Robust data security measures, such as encryption and access controls, should be in place to safeguard data from unauthorized access or cyber threats.

Data Integration: To provide a comprehensive view of the farm, data from different sensors and sources may need to be integrated. Data integration allows farmers to make more informed decisions by considering a wide range of variables.

In conclusion, agricultural sensors are the backbone of IoT in agriculture, playing a pivotal role in collecting real-time data that empowers farmers to make informed decisions. The various types of sensors employed in farming capture a wide range of data, from soil conditions to livestock behavior, providing a comprehensive view of the agricultural environment.

Effective data collection and management processes ensure that this wealth of information can be translated into actionable insights, resulting in more efficient and sustainable farming practices. In the following chapters, we will explore specific applications of agricultural sensors and their impact on various aspects of modern agriculture.

Chapter 3: IoT in Soil Monitoring and Analysis

Soil is the foundation of agriculture, and its health and condition play a pivotal role in determining crop yields and overall farm productivity. The integration of the Internet of Things (IoT) into soil monitoring and analysis has brought about a revolution in precision farming. This chapter explores the use of IoT in soil health monitoring, the technologies employed for nutrient and moisture sensing, and the implications for precision soil management.

Soil Health Monitoring with IoT

Soil health is a critical factor in modern agriculture, influencing crop growth, nutrient availability, and overall farm sustainability. Traditional methods of soil assessment, such as manual sampling and laboratory testing, have limitations in providing real-time data for decision-making. The advent of IoT technology has transformed soil monitoring into a dynamic and data-driven process.

IoT-enabled soil health monitoring involves the deployment of sensors and devices in the field that continuously collect data on various soil parameters. These parameters include soil moisture, temperature, pH levels, nutrient content, and even microbial activity. The real-time data collected is then transmitted to a central system, where it can be analyzed and interpreted by farmers and agricultural professionals.

The significance of IoT in soil health monitoring is underscored by the following key aspects:

Timely Insights: IoT sensors provide real-time data, enabling farmers to access information about their soil at any given moment. This is particularly valuable for making timely decisions, such as adjusting irrigation schedules to maintain optimal moisture levels or applying nutrients when soil conditions are favorable.

Data-Driven Precision: The continuous data collection and analysis facilitated by IoT technology enable data-driven precision in soil management. Farmers can fine-tune their practices based on accurate information, optimizing resource usage and crop growth.

Early Problem Detection: IoT sensors can detect early signs of soil issues, such as nutrient imbalances or pH fluctuations. Early detection allows farmers to take corrective actions before problems escalate and negatively impact crop health.

Sustainability: Precision soil monitoring contributes to sustainable farming practices by promoting efficient resource utilization. Farmers can minimize water wastage through precise irrigation and reduce the overuse of fertilizers and pesticides, which can harm the environment.

Nutrient and Moisture Sensing

Two critical aspects of soil health are nutrient levels and moisture content. IoT technology has introduced innovative solutions for monitoring these parameters in real-time, revolutionizing how farmers manage their soil and crops.

Nutrient Sensing: Nutrient sensors can measure the levels of essential elements in the soil, such as nitrogen, phosphorus, and potassium. These sensors employ various techniques, including electrical conductivity and spectroscopy, to assess nutrient content. The data generated by these sensors is crucial for optimizing fertilizer application. By tailoring nutrient inputs to the specific needs of the soil and crops, farmers can improve nutrient efficiency, reduce costs, and minimize nutrient runoff, which can have adverse effects on water bodies.

Moisture Sensing: Soil moisture sensors are fundamental in precision irrigation. They measure the moisture content of the soil at different depths, helping farmers determine when and how much to water their crops. IoT-based moisture sensors can offer precise, real-time data on soil moisture conditions. This information allows for the implementation of efficient irrigation practices, reducing water wastage and energy costs. Additionally, it prevents over-irrigation, which can lead to waterlogging and crop damage.

Combined Nutrient and Moisture Sensing: Some IoT sensors combine nutrient and moisture sensing capabilities in a single device. These multifunctional sensors provide a comprehensive view of the soil's condition, allowing for holistic soil management. By analyzing the interplay between soil moisture and nutrient levels, farmers can optimize irrigation and fertilization strategies to ensure healthy crop growth.

Precision Soil Management

The convergence of IoT technology with soil monitoring and analysis has paved the way for precision soil management, which is central to the concept of precision farming. This approach enables farmers to fine-tune their practices based on real-time data, resulting in optimized resource utilization and enhanced crop yields. Here are some key components and benefits of precision soil management:

Variable Rate Application: Precision soil management involves the use of variable rate technology (VRT) to apply resources such as fertilizers and pesticides at different rates across a field. VRT systems are guided by data from soil sensors, allowing farmers to customize their applications based on the specific needs of different areas within the same field. This approach minimizes resource waste, reduces environmental impact, and maximizes crop health.

Real-Time Decision-Making: With IoT-based soil monitoring, farmers can make decisions in real time. They receive immediate feedback from soil sensors, enabling them to respond quickly to changing conditions. For example, if a soil moisture sensor detects dry conditions in a certain area of a field, the irrigation system can be activated remotely to address the issue promptly.

Data Integration: Precision soil management systems often integrate data from multiple sources, including soil sensors, weather data, and historical records. This comprehensive data set provides a holistic view of the farm, allowing for more informed decision-making. For instance, the system can consider both soil moisture levels and weather forecasts to determine optimal irrigation timing.

Sustainability: Precision soil management contributes to sustainable agriculture by reducing the environmental impact of farming. Through more precise resource application, farmers can minimize the excess use of fertilizers and pesticides, which can leach into water bodies and harm ecosystems.

Additionally, efficient irrigation practices conserve water, a precious and increasingly scarce resource.

Crop Yield Optimization: Ultimately, the primary goal of precision soil management is to optimize crop yields. By tailoring farming practices to the specific needs of the soil and crops, farmers can achieve healthier and more productive plants. Increased crop yields are not only economically advantageous but also crucial for meeting the growing global demand for food.

In conclusion, IoT-driven soil monitoring and analysis have revolutionized the way farmers manage one of their most critical assets: soil. Through real-time data collection and analysis, IoT technology empowers farmers to make informed decisions, optimize resource utilization, and promote sustainable farming practices. Nutrient and moisture sensors, in particular, play a pivotal role in ensuring that crops receive the right amount of essential elements and water. The integration of these technologies leads to precision soil management, which is essential for modern agriculture's quest to produce more with fewer resources while minimizing environmental impact. Subsequent chapters will explore further applications of IoT in agriculture and its impact on various aspects of farming.

CHAPTER 4: IoT FOR CROP MONITORING

Crop monitoring is a fundamental component of precision farming, and the integration of the Internet of Things (IoT) has revolutionized how farmers assess the health of their crops. In this chapter, we explore how IoT technology enables crop health assessment, pest and disease detection, and the prediction of crop yields, providing farmers with valuable insights to optimize their agricultural practices.

Crop Health Assessment with IoT

Crop health is a critical factor in determining the success of any farming operation. The condition of crops can be affected by a multitude of factors, including soil quality, weather conditions, pest infestations, and disease outbreaks. Traditional methods of crop monitoring often rely on visual inspection, which may not provide a comprehensive or real-time assessment. IoT technology has brought about a paradigm shift in crop health assessment, allowing for continuous and data-driven monitoring.

The importance of IoT in crop health assessment can be understood through the following key aspects:

Real-Time Data Collection: IoT sensors and devices, such as drones and remote cameras, continuously collect data on crop conditions. This real-time data enables farmers to monitor their crops at all stages of growth and respond promptly to emerging issues.

Early Problem Detection: IoT-based crop monitoring systems can detect early signs of stress, nutrient deficiencies, or diseases. This early detection allows farmers to take preventive measures to mitigate the impact on crop yield and quality.

Data-Driven Decisions: The data collected by IoT sensors can be analyzed to gain valuable insights into crop health. These insights guide farmers in making data-driven decisions, such as adjusting irrigation schedules, modifying nutrient application, or implementing pest control measures.

Efficient Resource Utilization: IoT technology enables efficient resource utilization. By monitoring crop health in real time, farmers can tailor their practices to address specific issues in different parts of the field. This results in optimized resource use and reduced waste.

Environmental Sustainability: Precision crop health assessment contributes to environmental sustainability. By identifying problems early and applying treatments judiciously, farmers can minimize the need for chemical inputs, reducing the environmental impact of agriculture.

Pest and Disease Detection

Pest infestations and disease outbreaks can have devastating consequences for crops. Early detection and intervention are critical to mitigating the damage and preserving crop yield. IoT technology offers a range of tools and methods for the timely and accurate detection of pests and diseases.

Remote Sensing: IoT-enabled drones equipped with cameras and sensors can provide a bird's-eye view of the entire field. These drones capture high-resolution images that can be analyzed using machine learning algorithms to detect signs of stress or disease.

Changes in crop color, texture, or growth patterns can be indicative of pest infestations or diseases.

In-Field Sensors: IoT sensors can be deployed within the field to monitor conditions that are conducive to pest and disease development. For example, temperature and humidity sensors can alert farmers to conditions that favor the spread of certain plant pathogens. Soil moisture sensors can help identify areas where excess moisture may promote the growth of pests.

Image Recognition: IoT devices equipped with cameras and image recognition software can scan crops at a micro level to identify the presence of pests or diseases. This technology can distinguish between healthy and affected plants, enabling early intervention.

Data Analytics: IoT systems can integrate data from various sources, such as weather conditions, crop health data, and historical records, to predict the likelihood of pest or disease outbreaks. Predictive analytics can alert farmers to potential risks and help them plan for preemptive actions.

Wireless Alerts: IoT systems can send wireless alerts to farmers when unusual patterns or symptoms are detected in the field. Farmers can receive notifications on their mobile devices, allowing them to respond quickly to emerging threats.

Early detection of pests and diseases not only helps prevent crop damage but also reduces the need for broad-spectrum chemical treatments, promoting environmentally friendly farming practices.

Crop Yield Prediction

The ability to predict crop yields is of paramount importance for farmers, as it informs decisions related to marketing, logistics, and resource planning. IoT technology, when integrated with crop monitoring data, offers valuable insights for crop yield prediction.

Data Integration: IoT systems integrate data from multiple sources, including soil health, weather conditions, crop health, and historical data. This comprehensive data set provides a holistic view of the farm and its environment, allowing for more accurate yield predictions.

Machine Learning Algorithms: IoT-based crop monitoring systems often employ machine learning algorithms to analyze data patterns and make predictions. These algorithms can identify correlations between various factors and their impact on crop yield.

Historical Data: Historical crop data, such as past yields and farming practices, can be incorporated into the prediction models. This allows for the consideration of long-term trends and the impact of different management practices.

Real-Time Data Updates: IoT systems provide real-time updates on the conditions of the crops. As the growing season progresses, these updates can refine the predictions, accounting for changing environmental factors and crop development.

Risk Assessment: IoT technology can help farmers assess risks that may affect crop yield, such as weather events, disease outbreaks, or pest infestations. By identifying potential risks, farmers can take proactive measures to minimize their impact.

Decision Support: Crop yield predictions serve as a valuable decision support tool for farmers. They inform decisions related to harvest timing, storage, transportation, and marketing. Accurate predictions enable farmers to plan their resources more efficiently.

In conclusion, IoT technology has revolutionized crop monitoring by providing real-time data on crop health, enabling early pest and disease detection, and facilitating accurate crop yield predictions. These capabilities empower farmers to make informed decisions that optimize crop health, minimize losses, and enhance overall farm productivity.

The integration of IoT technology in crop monitoring represents a significant advancement in precision agriculture, which ultimately contributes to the sustainability and efficiency of modern farming practices. Subsequent chapters will explore additional applications of IoT in agriculture and their impact on various aspects of farming.

Chapter 5: IoT in Precision Irrigation

Irrigation is a cornerstone of agriculture, but water is a finite resource, and its efficient use is essential for sustainable farming. The integration of the Internet of Things (IoT) into precision irrigation has revolutionized how water is managed in agriculture. In this chapter, we will explore how IoT technology enables efficient water management, IoT-based irrigation systems, and water resource optimization.

Efficient Water Management with IoT

Water is a precious resource, and its responsible use is paramount in modern agriculture. In many regions of the world, water scarcity is a significant challenge, and in others, over-irrigation can lead to waterlogging, soil degradation, and environmental problems. IoT technology plays a pivotal role in efficient water management by enabling precise control of irrigation practices.

The significance of IoT in efficient water management can be understood through the following key aspects:

Real-Time Monitoring: IoT sensors, such as soil moisture sensors, weather stations, and remote cameras, continuously monitor environmental conditions and crop water needs. This real-time data allows farmers to assess when and how much water is required in specific areas of their fields.

Data-Driven Decision-Making: The data collected by IoT sensors is analyzed to provide actionable insights. Farmers can make informed decisions about when and how to irrigate based on accurate information, thus avoiding unnecessary water usage.

Precision Irrigation: IoT-based systems enable precision irrigation, where water is applied with high accuracy to meet the specific needs of crops. This approach minimizes over-irrigation, conserves water, and prevents waterlogging.

Automated Control: Many IoT-based irrigation systems are equipped with automation features. They can be programmed to adjust irrigation schedules based on preset thresholds and environmental conditions, such as soil moisture levels or weather forecasts.

Remote Monitoring: IoT technology enables remote monitoring and control of irrigation systems. Farmers can access real-time data and adjust irrigation settings from their smartphones or computers, regardless of their physical location.

Water Resource Efficiency: Efficient water management not only conserves water but also reduces energy costs associated with pumping and distributing water. This is especially relevant in regions where energy-intensive irrigation methods are used.

IoT-Based Irrigation Systems

IoT technology has brought forth a new era in irrigation systems, where precision and efficiency are paramount. These systems are designed to optimize water usage, reduce waste, and ensure that crops receive the right amount of water when they need it.

Soil Moisture Sensors: Soil moisture sensors are key components of IoT-based irrigation systems. They measure soil moisture at various depths and locations within the field. By continuously monitoring soil moisture levels, these sensors provide data that informs irrigation decisions. When soil moisture drops below a certain threshold, the system can trigger irrigation, ensuring that crops receive adequate water.

Weather Stations: Weather stations integrated with IoT systems provide real-time data on atmospheric conditions. This data is crucial for optimizing irrigation schedules. Farmers can adjust their irrigation plans based on weather forecasts, ensuring that water is applied when it's most beneficial for the crops.

Remote Control Systems: IoT-based irrigation systems often come with remote control features, allowing farmers to adjust irrigation settings from a distance. These systems can be accessed via a web interface or a mobile app, providing farmers with the flexibility to manage their irrigation practices in real time.

Automated Valves and Pumps: IoT technology can automate the operation of irrigation valves and pumps. These components can be controlled based on sensor data and programmed schedules, reducing the need for manual intervention.

Data Analytics and Decision Support: The data collected by IoT sensors and irrigation systems are analyzed to provide insights into irrigation efficiency and crop water needs. Decision support tools help farmers make informed choices about when and how to irrigate, optimizing water use.

Water Resource Optimization

Optimizing water resources in agriculture is not only about reducing consumption but also ensuring that water is distributed effectively to meet the needs of crops. IoT technology contributes to water resource optimization in various ways:

Tailored Irrigation: IoT-based systems enable precise irrigation tailored to the specific needs of crops. This ensures that water is applied at the right time and in the right amounts, enhancing crop health and yield.

Drip and Micro-Irrigation: IoT can support the implementation of drip and micro-irrigation systems, which deliver water directly to the root zone of plants. These systems minimize water loss due to evaporation and runoff, making irrigation more efficient.

Water Quality Management: IoT sensors can monitor the quality of water used for irrigation, ensuring that it is free from contaminants and suitable for agricultural use. Monitoring water quality prevents damage to crops and soil.

Monitoring Water Sources: IoT technology can be used to monitor the availability and levels of water sources, such as reservoirs and wells. This information is valuable for water resource planning and allocation.

Sustainability: By optimizing water use, IoT-based precision irrigation promotes sustainable farming practices. It reduces the environmental impact of agriculture, conserves water resources, and contributes to the overall efficiency and resilience of the farming operation.

IoT technology has ushered in a new era of efficient water management in agriculture through precision irrigation. The real-time monitoring of environmental conditions, data-driven decision-making, and the automation of irrigation systems have transformed the way farmers approach water use. By conserving water, minimizing waste, and ensuring that crops receive the right amount of moisture, IoT-based precision irrigation is an essential component of sustainable and efficient modern farming.

Chapter 6: IoT-Driven Pest and Disease Management

Pests and diseases pose significant threats to crop yields and can lead to substantial economic losses for farmers. The integration of the Internet of Things (IoT) has revolutionized pest and disease management in agriculture. In this chapter, we will explore how IoT technology enables early detection and diagnosis of pests and diseases, supports targeted pest control, and promotes sustainable pest management practices.

Early Detection and Diagnosis

Early detection and diagnosis of pests and diseases are crucial for effective pest management in agriculture. Recognizing these issues at their initial stages allows farmers to take timely and targeted actions to prevent widespread damage. IoT technology has introduced innovative solutions for early pest and disease detection.

The significance of IoT in early detection and diagnosis can be understood through the following key aspects:

Real-Time Monitoring: IoT sensors, cameras, and drones continuously monitor crops and their surroundings. Real-time data on crop health, environmental conditions, and pest presence are collected and transmitted to a central system for analysis.

Image Recognition: IoT systems use image recognition software to scan crops for signs of pests and diseases. Changes in crop color, texture, and growth patterns can be indicative of pest infestations or diseases. Machine learning algorithms can be employed to identify these visual cues.

Pest Traps and Monitoring: IoT devices can be equipped with pest traps and monitoring mechanisms. These traps use pheromones or other attractants to lure pests and monitor their activity. Data from the traps can indicate pest presence and help predict potential infestations.

Weather Data Integration: IoT systems can integrate real-time weather data, which is crucial for understanding how weather conditions may affect pest and disease patterns. Weather information can help predict the likelihood of pest outbreaks.

Wireless Alerts: IoT systems can send wireless alerts to farmers when unusual patterns or symptoms are detected in the field. These alerts serve as early warnings that prompt farmers to investigate and take appropriate actions.

Historical Data Analysis: IoT systems can analyze historical data on pest and disease occurrences and relate them to specific environmental conditions. This helps in predicting the likelihood of outbreaks based on previous patterns.

Disease Diagnosis Support: IoT systems can assist with disease diagnosis by analyzing visual symptoms and matching them to a database of known diseases. This can aid in confirming disease outbreaks and facilitating the selection of appropriate treatment measures.

Early detection and diagnosis enabled by IoT technology not only save time and resources but also significantly reduce the use of pesticides, promoting environmentally friendly and sustainable farming practices.

IoT for Targeted Pest Control

Traditional pest control methods often involve blanket applications of pesticides, which can be harmful to the environment, non-target species, and even humans. IoT technology offers targeted pest control solutions, reducing the need for broad-spectrum chemical treatments.

The significance of IoT in targeted pest control can be understood through the following key aspects:

Precision Pest Identification: IoT systems can precisely identify the type of pest infesting a crop. This knowledge allows farmers to select and apply specific pest control measures that are effective against the identified pest while sparing beneficial insects.

Automated Pest Traps: IoT-based pest traps can be programmed to release pesticides only when a threshold of pest activity is detected. This automation minimizes pesticide use and ensures that treatments are applied when and where they are most needed.

Drones for Precision Spraying: Drones equipped with IoT technology can be used for targeted pesticide spraying. These drones can follow predetermined flight paths, releasing pesticides only in areas with confirmed pest infestations, sparing unaffected crops.

Release of Beneficial Organisms: IoT technology can aid in the release of beneficial organisms, such as ladybugs or parasitoid wasps, which naturally control pest populations. These releases can be precisely timed and targeted based on pest activity.

Monitoring Pest Thresholds: IoT sensors and traps can monitor pest thresholds and send alerts to farmers when pest levels reach a critical point. This enables farmers to initiate pest control measures at the right moment to prevent crop damage.

Reduced Pesticide Residues: By minimizing the use of pesticides, IoT-based targeted pest control reduces the risk of pesticide residues on crops, making produce safer for consumption.

Sustainable Pest Management

Sustainable pest management practices are essential for minimizing the environmental impact of agriculture and ensuring long-term food security. IoT technology has played a pivotal role in promoting sustainable pest management in several ways:

Reduced Chemical Use: The precision and accuracy of IoT-enabled pest control methods reduce the need for chemical pesticides. This minimizes the negative impact on non-target species and reduces chemical residues in soil and water.

Increased Crop Resilience: Sustainable pest management practices focus on building crop resilience through methods like crop rotation, intercropping, and the use of resistant plant varieties. IoT technology can help farmers implement these practices more effectively.

Monitoring Environmental Impact: IoT sensors and systems can monitor the environmental impact of pest control measures. For example, they can assess the impact of pesticide runoff on water bodies or the effects of pest management on beneficial insect populations.

Ecosystem Preservation: Sustainable pest management aims to preserve natural ecosystems and biodiversity. IoT-based targeted pest control methods are less harmful to beneficial insects, which are essential for pollination and maintaining ecological balance.

Adaptive Pest Management: IoT systems can provide data that supports adaptive pest management. Farmers can adjust their pest control strategies in response to changing conditions, pest resistance, or emerging threats.

Economic Efficiency: Sustainable pest management practices can reduce costs associated with pest control. For example, the targeted application of pesticides or the release of beneficial organisms can be cost-effective.

In conclusion, IoT technology has brought about a transformation in pest and disease management in agriculture. Early detection and diagnosis, targeted pest control, and sustainable pest management practices have become more accessible and effective through IoT systems. This not only reduces the negative impact of agriculture on the environment but also promotes sustainable and efficient farming practices. In the following chapters, we will delve into additional applications of IoT in agriculture and explore their impact on various aspects of the industry.

Chapter 7: IoT for Crop Nutrition

Nutrition is a critical factor in crop growth, and the proper management of nutrients is essential for achieving healthy and high-yielding crops. The integration of the Internet of Things (IoT) has revolutionized crop nutrition in agriculture. In this chapter, we will explore how IoT technology enables nutrient monitoring and optimization, supports IoT-enhanced fertilization, and promotes sustainable crop nutrition practices.

Nutrient Monitoring and Optimization

Effective nutrient management is central to modern agriculture. The balanced supply of essential nutrients, such as nitrogen, phosphorus, and potassium, is vital for crop growth and development. Insufficient or excessive nutrient levels can result in reduced yields and environmental issues. IoT technology has introduced advanced solutions for nutrient monitoring and optimization.

The significance of IoT in nutrient monitoring and optimization can be understood through the following key aspects:

Real-Time Nutrient Monitoring: IoT sensors continuously monitor nutrient levels in the soil, providing real-time data on the availability of essential elements. This information is essential for optimizing nutrient application.

Data-Driven Decision-Making: The data collected by IoT sensors is analyzed to provide insights into nutrient levels and their impact on crop health. This data-driven approach allows farmers to make informed decisions regarding nutrient management.

Nutrient Targeting: IoT-based systems enable precision nutrient targeting, where nutrients are applied only in areas where they are needed. This minimizes over-fertilization and reduces the risk of nutrient runoff into water bodies.

Dynamic Nutrient Adjustments: IoT technology allows for dynamic adjustments to nutrient applications based on real-time data. Farmers can fine-tune nutrient levels as crop needs change throughout the growing season.

Remote Monitoring: IoT systems often offer remote monitoring and control features, allowing farmers to access nutrient data and adjust applications from their smartphones or computers.

Historical Data Analysis: IoT systems can analyze historical data to identify nutrient trends and patterns. This historical perspective can inform nutrient management strategies.

IoT-Enhanced Fertilization

Fertilization is a fundamental practice in agriculture, and IoT technology has introduced innovative methods to enhance the efficiency of nutrient application. IoT-enhanced fertilization aims to provide crops with the right nutrients at the right time and in the right quantities.

The significance of IoT in enhancing fertilization can be understood through the following key aspects:

Variable Rate Fertilization: IoT technology enables variable rate technology (VRT) for fertilization. VRT systems use data from IoT sensors to adjust nutrient application rates across a field. This precision approach ensures that each area of the field receives the optimal amount of nutrients.

Nutrient Mapping: IoT systems can create nutrient maps of fields, indicating areas with nutrient deficiencies or excesses. These maps guide VRT systems to apply nutrients according to the specific needs of each area.

Remote Control: IoT-enhanced fertilization systems offer remote control features. Farmers can remotely adjust and monitor the operation of fertilizer application equipment, ensuring precise nutrient delivery.

Real-Time Data Integration: IoT technology integrates real-time data, including weather conditions, soil moisture, and crop health, into the fertilization process. This data informs decisions about when and how to apply nutrients.

Adaptive Fertilization: IoT technology allows for adaptive fertilization. Fertilization plans can be adjusted based on changing environmental conditions or crop growth stages.

Reduced Nutrient Loss: IoT-enhanced fertilization reduces the risk of nutrient loss to the environment, such as nutrient runoff into water bodies. By applying nutrients only where they are needed, excess application and subsequent runoff are minimized.

Sustainable Crop Nutrition

Sustainable crop nutrition is a cornerstone of modern agriculture, aiming to balance the needs of crops with environmental responsibility. IoT technology contributes to sustainable crop nutrition practices in several ways:

Reduced Nutrient Waste: IoT technology minimizes nutrient waste by applying nutrients with precision. This approach reduces over-fertilization, which can result in nutrient runoff and environmental pollution.

Environmental Impact Monitoring: IoT systems can monitor the environmental impact of fertilization, such as nutrient runoff or emissions of greenhouse gases. This data allows farmers to make adjustments to minimize their environmental footprint.

Carbon Footprint Reduction: By optimizing nutrient application and minimizing the need for excess fertilizers, IoT-enhanced fertilization can reduce the carbon footprint of agriculture.

Water Quality Preservation: Sustainable crop nutrition practices promoted by IoT technology help preserve water quality by minimizing nutrient runoff into water bodies, which can lead to algal blooms and ecosystem damage.

Soil Health Improvement: Sustainable crop nutrition aims to enhance soil health by maintaining nutrient balance and preventing soil degradation. IoT technology supports these goals by optimizing nutrient management.

Economic Efficiency: Sustainable crop nutrition practices are often economically efficient. By applying nutrients more precisely and minimizing waste, farmers can reduce fertilizer costs.

Regulatory Compliance: IoT-enhanced fertilization practices help farmers comply with environmental regulations and standards related to nutrient management.

Chapter 8: Farm Equipment Automation with IoT

Farm equipment automation is a game-changer in modern agriculture, offering increased efficiency, reduced labor costs, and improved precision in farming operations. The integration of the Internet of Things (IoT) has played a pivotal role in advancing the capabilities of farm machinery. In this chapter, we will explore the role of IoT in autonomous farm machinery, smart farming equipment, and IoT in precision farming drones.

Autonomous Farm Machinery

Autonomous farm machinery, commonly referred to as self-driving or driverless equipment, is one of the most significant innovations in agriculture. These machines can perform various tasks without human intervention, ranging from planting and harvesting to weeding and soil preparation. IoT technology is at the heart of this agricultural revolution, enabling real-time data collection, analysis, and decision-making for autonomous machinery.

The significance of IoT in autonomous farm machinery can be understood through the following key aspects:

Real-Time Data Sensors: IoT-equipped autonomous machinery is equipped with various sensors that monitor environmental conditions, soil health, and crop status. These sensors collect data and transmit it to the central system for real-time analysis.

GPS and Navigation Systems: GPS technology, coupled with IoT, provides precise positioning and navigation for autonomous machinery. This allows machines to follow predefined routes and adjust their operations based on field conditions.

Remote Monitoring and Control: Farmers can remotely monitor the progress and status of autonomous machinery through IoT systems. They can also make real-time adjustments or intervene when necessary.

Data-Driven Decision-Making: IoT systems analyze the data collected by autonomous machinery to make informed decisions about crop and soil management. This results in more efficient and optimized farming practices.

Reduced Labor Costs: Autonomous machinery reduces the need for manual labor, resulting in cost savings for farmers. It also mitigates labor shortages, a common issue in agriculture.

Increased Precision: IoT technology enhances the precision of autonomous machinery. It can identify and respond to variations in soil and crop conditions, ensuring that operations are tailored to specific areas within a field.

Smart Farming Equipment

Smart farming equipment goes beyond autonomy and involves various connected devices that collect and transmit data to improve farm management. IoT technology plays a fundamental role in making farming equipment "smart." Here are some key aspects of IoT in smart farming equipment:

Remote Monitoring: IoT-connected devices on farm equipment, such as tractors, plows, and sprayers, enable remote monitoring. Farmers can track the location, status, and performance of equipment in real-time.

Predictive Maintenance: IoT sensors can monitor the condition of machinery components, such as engines and gears. By collecting data on factors like temperature and vibration, predictive maintenance alerts can be generated, preventing breakdowns and reducing downtime.

Efficiency Optimization: Data collected from smart equipment can help farmers optimize operational efficiency. This includes monitoring fuel consumption, engine performance, and equipment utilization.

Automation Integration: Smart farming equipment can be integrated into automation processes. For example, tractors equipped with GPS and IoT technology can follow predefined paths, reducing the need for manual guidance.

Data Analysis: IoT systems process and analyze the data collected by smart equipment. This data can inform decisions about crop management, resource allocation, and equipment usage.

Sustainability: Smart farming equipment promotes sustainability by optimizing resource use. By minimizing inputs like fuel and water, it reduces the environmental impact of farming.

Precision Farming: Smart farming equipment supports precision farming practices by enabling accurate planting, harvesting, and spraying, tailored to specific field conditions.

IoT in Precision Farming Drones

Drones have become valuable tools in precision farming, enabling farmers to monitor crops and fields from the air. When combined with IoT technology, drones provide real-time data on crop health, nutrient status, and pest infestations. Here are the key aspects of IoT in precision farming drones:

Remote Sensing: IoT-equipped drones are equipped with various sensors, such as multispectral and thermal cameras. These sensors capture data on crop conditions, moisture levels, and temperature variations.

Real-Time Data Transmission: Drones collect data during their flights and transmit it in real-time to the central system. This data is crucial for timely decision-making in crop management.

Image Recognition: IoT systems process the images and data collected by drones to identify crop stress, nutrient deficiencies, and potential pest or disease outbreaks. Machine learning algorithms can be employed to analyze images and recognize patterns.

Targeted Actions: Once issues are detected, IoT systems can guide farmers in taking targeted actions. For example, if a drone identifies areas with dry soil, it can prompt farmers to adjust irrigation in those specific zones.

GPS and Navigation: Drones equipped with GPS and IoT technology can follow predefined flight paths, covering the entire field or focusing on specific areas of interest. This ensures comprehensive data collection.

Environmental Monitoring: Drones can monitor and assess environmental conditions that may impact crops, such as temperature, humidity, and wind speed. This data informs decisions related to crop protection and management.

Reduced Resource Usage: IoT-connected drones enhance resource efficiency by providing precise information about where resources are needed most. This minimizes the overuse of water, fertilizers, and pesticides.

Safety and Scalability: Drones provide a safe and scalable means of monitoring large agricultural areas. They can access remote or difficult-to-reach areas, reducing the need for manual inspections.

In conclusion, IoT technology has ushered in a new era of automation and smart equipment in agriculture. Autonomous machinery, smart farming equipment, and IoT-equipped drones have transformed the way farmers manage their operations. These technologies improve efficiency, reduce labor costs, increase precision, and promote sustainability in agriculture. In the following chapters, we will explore additional applications of IoT in agriculture and their impact on various aspects of the industry.

CHAPTER 9: IoT FOR WEATHER FORECASTING

Weather is a critical factor in agriculture, impacting decisions related to planting, irrigation, harvesting, and pest management. The integration of the Internet of Things (IoT) has revolutionized the field of weather forecasting in agriculture. In this chapter, we will explore the role of IoT in weather stations for agriculture, IoT-enhanced weather predictions, and weather-based decision support.

IoT Weather Stations and Agriculture

Weather stations have long been used in agriculture to collect data on atmospheric conditions, temperature, humidity, wind speed, and precipitation. However, traditional weather stations often provide data at limited intervals and locations. IoT technology has expanded the capabilities of weather stations, making real-time data collection and monitoring a reality.

The significance of IoT in weather stations for agriculture can be understood through the following key aspects:

Real-Time Data Collection: IoT weather stations continuously collect data on a range of atmospheric parameters. This real-time data is transmitted wirelessly and is available for analysis and decision-making.

Localized Information: IoT weather stations can be strategically placed throughout a farm to provide localized weather information. This granular data allows farmers to make site-specific decisions about their crops and operations.

Custom Sensors: IoT technology allows for the integration of custom sensors that measure specific parameters relevant to agriculture. For example, soil moisture sensors can be added to provide comprehensive environmental data.

Remote Monitoring: Farmers can access weather data remotely through IoT systems, allowing them to monitor conditions even when they are not on the farm. This remote access is valuable for making timely decisions.

Weather Alerts: IoT weather stations can send alerts to farmers when specific conditions, such as frost or heavy rain, are detected. These alerts prompt farmers to take protective actions for their crops.

Historical Data Analysis: IoT systems store historical weather data, enabling farmers to analyze weather patterns and trends. This information is valuable for long-term planning and decision-making.

IoT-Enhanced Weather Predictions

Weather predictions are essential for farmers to plan their planting, harvesting, and irrigation schedules. IoT technology enhances the accuracy and reliability of weather forecasts, providing real-time data that complements traditional meteorological models.

The significance of IoT in enhancing weather predictions can be understood through the following key aspects:

Data Fusion: IoT technology combines data from various sources, including weather stations, satellites, and environmental sensors. This data fusion improves the accuracy of weather predictions by providing a more comprehensive picture of atmospheric conditions.

Real-Time Data: IoT systems collect real-time data that can be integrated into weather models. This data includes information on temperature, humidity, wind, and precipitation, which are critical for forecasting.

Localized Forecasts: IoT technology allows for localized weather forecasting. By considering real-time data from IoT weather stations, forecasts can be customized for specific regions, ensuring that farmers receive accurate predictions for their locations.

High-Resolution Models: IoT-enhanced weather predictions can provide high-resolution models that offer more detailed information about weather patterns. This is particularly valuable for precision farming, where decisions are made at the field level.

Timely Updates: IoT systems can provide timely updates on weather forecasts, enabling farmers to adjust their plans as conditions change. For example, if heavy rain is predicted, farmers can postpone field operations to prevent soil compaction.

Climate Data: IoT technology incorporates historical climate data into weather predictions, allowing for long-term climate modeling. This helps farmers anticipate climate-related challenges and make informed decisions.

Weather-Based Decision Support

Weather-based decision support systems are a valuable tool for farmers, helping them make informed choices about crop management, resource allocation, and risk mitigation. IoT technology plays a central role in providing the data necessary for weather-based decision support.

The significance of IoT in weather-based decision support can be understood through the following key aspects:

Crop Management: IoT weather data informs decisions related to crop management. For example, farmers can adjust irrigation schedules based on predicted rainfall or protect crops from frost when low temperatures are forecasted.

Pest and Disease Management: Weather predictions and data from IoT weather stations can guide pest and disease management practices. For instance, farmers can time pesticide applications based on pest life cycles and weather conditions.

Water Resource Allocation: Weather-based decision support helps farmers optimize water resource allocation. When drought conditions are predicted, farmers can prioritize irrigation for high-value crops.

Risk Mitigation: IoT-enhanced weather data enables farmers to assess and mitigate risks. For instance, if severe weather, such as a hailstorm, is predicted, farmers can take protective measures to minimize crop damage.

Yield Optimization: Weather-based decision support systems help farmers optimize crop yields. By aligning planting and harvesting schedules with favorable weather conditions, farmers can maximize their productivity.

Environmental Sustainability: Weather-based decision support supports environmentally sustainable farming practices. By avoiding unnecessary resource use and aligning operations with weather forecasts, farmers reduce their environmental impact.

Economic Efficiency: Making informed decisions based on weather data reduces waste, increases efficiency, and minimizes costs. It also promotes the responsible use of resources.

Insurance and Risk Management: Weather data is invaluable for agricultural insurance and risk management. IoT-enhanced weather predictions enable insurers to assess and price risks accurately, benefiting both farmers and the insurance industry.

In conclusion, IoT technology has transformed weather forecasting and decision support in agriculture. IoT weather stations provide real-time data on atmospheric conditions, while IoT-enhanced weather predictions offer high-resolution and localized forecasts. Weather-based decision support systems empower farmers to make informed choices about crop management, resource allocation, and risk mitigation. This results in more efficient, sustainable, and economically viable agricultural practices. In the subsequent chapters, we will delve into additional applications of IoT in agriculture and explore their impact on various aspects of the industry.

CHAPTER 10: IoT IN LIVESTOCK MANAGEMENT

Livestock farming is a significant sector of agriculture, and the integration of the Internet of Things (IoT) has brought about transformative changes in livestock management. IoT technology plays a pivotal role in smart livestock monitoring, ensuring the health and well-being of farm animals, and optimizing efficiency in livestock farming practices. In this chapter, we will explore how IoT is revolutionizing the way farmers manage their livestock.

Smart Livestock Monitoring

Smart livestock monitoring is a key application of IoT technology in agriculture. It involves the use of sensors, tracking devices, and data analytics to monitor the behavior, health, and performance of farm animals. This real-time data enables farmers to make informed decisions, enhance animal well-being, and improve overall farm productivity.

The significance of IoT in smart livestock monitoring can be understood through the following key aspects:

Real-Time Data Collection: IoT sensors and devices continuously collect data on various parameters, such as animal movement, temperature, and feeding patterns. This real-time data provides insights into the health and behavior of livestock.

Animal Identification: IoT technology enables the use of RFID tags, ear tags, or other identification methods to track individual animals. This facilitates the monitoring of each animal's health and performance.

Location Tracking: GPS-based IoT systems can track the location of animals, preventing them from straying or getting lost. This is particularly valuable for extensive grazing systems.

Environmental Monitoring: IoT sensors can monitor environmental conditions within livestock facilities, such as temperature, humidity, and air quality. This ensures that animals are kept in comfortable and healthy surroundings.

Disease Detection: IoT technology can identify signs of disease or distress in animals, enabling early intervention and disease control. Changes in behavior, temperature, or other vital signs can trigger alerts.

Reproduction and Breeding Management: IoT systems can provide insights into the reproductive health and breeding cycles of livestock. This helps farmers optimize breeding programs.

Feeding and Nutrition: IoT sensors can track feeding patterns and nutrition intake. This data is valuable for assessing the dietary needs of individual animals and optimizing feed usage.

Remote Monitoring: Farmers can access real-time data and receive alerts remotely, ensuring that livestock are monitored around the clock.

Health and Well-being of Farm Animals

The health and well-being of farm animals are paramount in livestock management. IoT technology empowers farmers to proactively monitor and care for their animals, promoting better health and higher productivity.

The significance of IoT in ensuring the health and well-being of farm animals can be understood through the following key aspects:

Disease Prevention: IoT technology can help prevent disease outbreaks by monitoring animal behavior and health parameters. Early detection of illness allows for prompt isolation and treatment.

Vaccination Management: IoT systems can track vaccination schedules for each animal, ensuring that they receive timely immunizations and preventive care.

Weight and Growth Monitoring: IoT sensors can monitor the weight and growth of animals, allowing farmers to assess their overall health and nutritional needs.

Heat Stress Mitigation: IoT sensors can detect signs of heat stress in livestock and trigger cooling systems or other interventions to prevent heat-related health issues.

Reproductive Health: IoT technology assists in monitoring the reproductive health of animals, enabling farmers to optimize breeding programs and ensure successful pregnancies.

Behavioral Analytics: Changes in animal behavior can indicate health issues or distress. IoT systems use behavioral analytics to identify deviations from normal patterns.

Stress Reduction: IoT technology can support stress reduction measures, such as automated feed dispensers, comfortable living conditions, and appropriate lighting.

Labor Efficiency: By automating health monitoring and management, IoT technology reduces the need for manual inspections and interventions, freeing up labor for other tasks.

Animal Welfare Compliance: IoT systems help farmers comply with animal welfare standards and regulations by providing data on animal care and well-being.

IoT for Efficient Livestock Farming

Efficiency is a critical factor in modern livestock farming. IoT technology optimizes various aspects of livestock management to improve overall farm efficiency, reduce costs, and increase productivity.

The significance of IoT in efficient livestock farming can be understood through the following key aspects:

Resource Optimization: IoT technology supports the efficient use of resources, including feed, water, and energy. For example, automated feeders and waterers can dispense precise amounts based on the needs of individual animals.

Data-Driven Decision-Making: Real-time data collected by IoT systems informs decisions about animal health, breeding, feeding, and overall management. This data-driven approach leads to more efficient and informed choices.

Waste Reduction: IoT technology minimizes waste by providing insights into resource consumption and optimizing resource allocation. This reduces the environmental impact of livestock farming.

Labor Savings: Automation and remote monitoring reduce the need for manual labor in livestock management. Labor efficiency is increased, and labor costs are reduced.

Precision Breeding: IoT technology allows for precise breeding management, ensuring that animals with the best genetics are selected for breeding. This improves the quality of livestock.

Productivity Enhancement: Real-time data on animal health and nutrition enables farmers to optimize productivity. Healthier and well-fed animals result in higher yields and better-quality products.

Data Analytics: IoT systems analyze historical data to identify trends and patterns. This historical perspective helps farmers make informed decisions about livestock management.

Sustainability: Efficient livestock farming practices promoted by IoT technology contribute to environmental sustainability. They minimize the environmental impact of livestock farming and reduce resource consumption.

Risk Mitigation: IoT technology helps farmers mitigate risks by providing early warning signs of health issues or environmental conditions that may impact livestock.

In conclusion, IoT technology has brought transformative changes to livestock management in agriculture. Smart livestock monitoring ensures that animals are healthy and well-cared for, while IoT systems support efficiency and resource optimization in livestock farming. These technologies empower farmers to make informed decisions, reduce costs, and promote sustainable and productive livestock farming practices. In the subsequent chapters, we will delve into additional applications of IoT in agriculture and explore their impact on various aspects of the industry.

Chapter 11: Sustainability and Environmental Impact

Sustainability and reducing the environmental impact of agriculture are pressing concerns in our rapidly changing world. Agriculture is both a critical industry for food production and a significant contributor to environmental challenges such as greenhouse gas emissions, water usage, and soil degradation.

The integration of the Internet of Things (IoT) has emerged as a powerful tool for promoting sustainable agriculture practices and mitigating the environmental footprint of farming. In this chapter, we will explore the role of IoT in sustainable agriculture practices, reducing the environmental impact, and IoT solutions for conservation.

Sustainable Agriculture Practices with IoT

Sustainable agriculture practices prioritize long-term environmental, economic, and social viability. IoT technology supports a range of sustainability initiatives in agriculture by providing real-time data and decision-making tools that enable farmers to make informed choices about resource management and crop production. Some key areas where IoT enhances sustainability in agriculture include:

Precision Agriculture: IoT sensors and devices enable precision farming by providing real-time data on soil conditions, weather patterns, and crop health. This allows farmers to optimize the use of resources such as water, fertilizers, and pesticides, reducing waste and environmental impact.

Irrigation Management: IoT-based irrigation systems use data from weather forecasts, soil moisture sensors, and evapotranspiration models to tailor watering schedules and reduce water waste. By avoiding over-irrigation, this technology conserves a precious resource and lowers energy costs.

Soil Health Monitoring: IoT sensors assess soil quality, nutrient levels, and erosion risks. Farmers can adjust land management practices based on this data to protect the long-term health of their soil and reduce the need for synthetic inputs.

Pest and Disease Management: IoT technology supports sustainable pest management by offering real-time data on pest presence and behavior. This allows farmers to implement targeted, reduced-risk pest control measures, minimizing the use of pesticides.

Biodiversity Conservation: IoT devices can monitor biodiversity and ecosystems on farmland, helping farmers identify areas for habitat conservation and providing data for wildlife-friendly agricultural practices.

Carbon Footprint Reduction: IoT technology enables the monitoring of energy consumption and greenhouse gas emissions. This data supports energy-efficient and low-carbon farming practices, which reduce the environmental impact of agriculture.

Water Quality Preservation: IoT systems can monitor and manage water quality in irrigation and runoff, minimizing contamination and protecting aquatic ecosystems.

Organic Farming: IoT technology supports the management of organic farming practices, which focus on reducing synthetic chemical inputs, conserving resources, and fostering biodiversity.

Sustainable Crop Rotation: IoT data can inform decisions about crop rotation, cover cropping, and agroforestry systems, which promote soil health and pest management while reducing the need for synthetic inputs.

Reducing the Environmental Footprint

The environmental footprint of agriculture includes a range of impacts, such as greenhouse gas emissions, water usage, soil erosion, and chemical pollution. IoT technology is helping to mitigate these environmental effects by providing data-driven insights that guide more responsible agricultural practices. Some key areas of impact reduction include:

Precision Resource Management: IoT-based precision agriculture minimizes the overuse of resources like water, fertilizers, and pesticides. This reduces waste and environmental pollution, lowering the overall environmental footprint.

Reduced Carbon Emissions: IoT technology enables more efficient farming practices, reducing energy consumption and associated carbon emissions. Additionally, IoT supports the monitoring of carbon sequestration in soil and vegetation.

Water Conservation: IoT-driven precision irrigation reduces water waste and conserves this critical resource. By avoiding excessive watering and managing runoff, it also safeguards water bodies from contamination.

Soil Conservation: IoT sensors and devices promote soil health and reduce soil erosion. These measures protect topsoil and prevent sediment runoff into water bodies, which can be detrimental to aquatic ecosystems.

Pesticide Minimization: IoT-based pest and disease management practices minimize the use of pesticides, reducing chemical pollution in soil and water. This also helps preserve beneficial insect populations and promotes ecosystem balance.

Sustainable Energy Use: IoT technology enables the monitoring of energy consumption on farms. By identifying energy-efficient practices and equipment, farmers can reduce their energy footprint.

Sustainable Land Use: IoT supports land use planning that prioritizes the preservation of natural habitats and open spaces. By avoiding the expansion of farmland into sensitive areas, this technology protects biodiversity.

Waste Reduction: IoT data can help reduce waste on farms by optimizing resource allocation and minimizing overproduction. This reduces the need for waste disposal and lowers the environmental impact.

Reduced Soil Degradation: IoT-supported soil management practices reduce soil degradation and maintain soil fertility. Healthy soils are more resilient to erosion and better at sequestering carbon.

IoT Solutions for Conservation

Conservation efforts in agriculture focus on protecting natural habitats, biodiversity, and ecosystem services. IoT technology plays a crucial role in these efforts by providing data and tools to support conservation practices. Some key applications of IoT in agricultural conservation include:

Habitat Monitoring: IoT sensors and cameras monitor wildlife populations, nesting sites, and migratory patterns. This data informs habitat conservation strategies and the protection of critical ecosystems on farmland.

Erosion Control: IoT systems provide real-time data on soil conditions, erosion risks, and land management practices. This data guides erosion control measures, such as cover cropping and no-till farming.

Water Quality Preservation: IoT technology monitors water quality in water bodies adjacent to farmland. This data helps identify potential pollution sources and supports water quality conservation efforts.

Invasive Species Management: IoT devices track the presence and behavior of invasive species. This information informs targeted eradication efforts, protecting native flora and fauna.

Pollinator Conservation: IoT sensors monitor pollinator activity and behavior, aiding in the conservation of pollinators critical to crop production.

Wildlife-Friendly Farming: IoT data helps farmers implement wildlife-friendly agricultural practices. For example, it can guide the planting of cover crops to provide food and habitat for birds and other wildlife.

Conservation Easements: IoT technology can be used to monitor and enforce conservation easements on farmland, ensuring that protected areas remain intact.

Carbon Sequestration: IoT systems track the sequestration of carbon in soil and vegetation. This information supports carbon credit programs and encourages the conservation of natural carbon sinks.

Biodiversity Data Collection: IoT devices collect data on biodiversity and ecosystem services provided by natural areas on farms. This data informs conservation decisions and highlights the value of these areas.

In conclusion, IoT technology has become a powerful tool for promoting sustainability and reducing the environmental impact of agriculture. From precision resource management to environmental impact reduction and conservation efforts, IoT is instrumental in advancing responsible farming practices. These applications not only protect the environment but also contribute to long-term food security and the well-being of our planet. In the following chapters, we will delve into additional applications of IoT in agriculture and explore their impact on various aspects of the industry.

Chapter 12: Challenges and Future Trends in IoT Agriculture

As the adoption of the Internet of Things (IoT) in agriculture continues to grow, the industry faces both opportunities and challenges. In this chapter, we will explore the challenges that need to be overcome to fully realize the potential of IoT in agriculture, the upcoming innovations and future possibilities, and how the industry can prepare for the next generation of precision farming.

Overcoming Challenges in IoT Adoption

The integration of IoT technology in agriculture has brought numerous benefits, but it has also presented its share of challenges. Addressing these challenges is essential for the continued success and widespread adoption of IoT in farming. Some of the key challenges in IoT adoption in agriculture include:

High Initial Costs: The deployment of IoT infrastructure, including sensors, data networks, and analytics platforms, can be expensive. Small and resource-constrained farmers may find it challenging to invest in these technologies. To overcome this, there is a need for cost-effective and scalable solutions, as well as financial support mechanisms for small-scale farmers.

Data Privacy and Security: IoT devices collect sensitive data related to crop yields, weather conditions, and farm operations. Protecting this data from cyber threats and ensuring privacy is a significant challenge. Robust security measures and data encryption are necessary to safeguard farmers' data.

Interoperability: The diversity of IoT devices and platforms can lead to compatibility issues. Ensuring that different sensors and systems can communicate and share data effectively is vital. Standardization efforts are ongoing to address this challenge.

Connectivity: In remote or rural areas, reliable internet connectivity may be limited. IoT devices rely on connectivity to transmit data and receive updates, making connectivity a fundamental challenge. Expanding network coverage and exploring alternative connectivity solutions are necessary steps.

Data Management: IoT generates a vast amount of data that needs to be managed, processed, and analyzed effectively. Handling large datasets can be challenging, and there is a need for user-friendly data management solutions and data analytics tools.

Energy Efficiency: Many IoT devices in agriculture are powered by batteries or solar panels. Ensuring the long-term energy efficiency and sustainability of these devices is a challenge. Research into low-power technologies and energy harvesting solutions is ongoing.

User Training and Adoption: Farmers and agricultural workers need to be trained to effectively use IoT technology. This challenge can be addressed through training programs, user-friendly interfaces, and support services.

Data Ownership and Control: Farmers need to have control over the data generated by IoT devices on their farms. Ensuring that data ownership and control are clearly defined in agreements with technology providers is essential.

Upcoming Innovations and Future Possibilities

The future of IoT in agriculture holds promising innovations that have the potential to address current challenges and open up new possibilities. Some of the upcoming innovations and trends in IoT agriculture include:

5G Connectivity: The rollout of 5G networks promises faster and more reliable connectivity, which is crucial for IoT devices. This will enable real-time data transmission and support applications like remote-controlled farm machinery and augmented reality for farm management.

Artificial Intelligence (AI) Integration: The combination of IoT and AI allows for more advanced data analysis and decision-making. AI-driven predictive analytics can provide actionable insights and recommendations for farmers to optimize their operations.

Blockchain for Supply Chain Transparency: Blockchain technology can be used to create transparent and secure supply chains for agricultural products. Consumers can trace the origin of food products, and farmers can receive fair compensation for their produce.

Smart Farming Ecosystems: Integrated ecosystems of IoT devices, including sensors, drones, and robotics, will become more common. These ecosystems will work together to perform tasks like crop monitoring, irrigation, and pest control more efficiently.

**Automated Farming: ** The integration of IoT and automation technologies will lead to more autonomous farm machinery. Self-driving tractors and robotic harvesters can perform tasks with minimal human intervention, reducing labor costs and increasing efficiency.

Edge Computing: IoT devices are becoming more powerful and capable of processing data at the edge of the network, reducing the need to transmit all data to the cloud. Edge computing enables real-time decision-making and reduces data transmission costs.

Environmental Monitoring: IoT sensors and devices will play a crucial role in monitoring and mitigating the environmental impact of agriculture. This includes tracking carbon sequestration, monitoring water quality, and preserving natural habitats on farmland.

Biotechnology Integration: IoT can be combined with biotechnology to develop precision breeding and genetically modified crops that are more resilient to changing climate conditions and pests.

Data-Driven Farm Management: Data-driven decision support systems will become more sophisticated, providing farmers with insights into crop management, resource allocation, and risk mitigation. These systems will be powered by advanced analytics and machine learning.

Preparing for the Next Generation of Precision Farming

To prepare for the next generation of precision farming driven by IoT technology, several key steps are essential:

Investment in Infrastructure: Farmers and agricultural organizations should invest in the necessary IoT infrastructure, including sensors, communication networks, and data management systems.

Public-private partnerships can facilitate these investments, especially for small-scale farmers.

Education and Training: Training programs and resources should be made available to help farmers and agricultural workers understand how to use IoT technology effectively. This includes training in data analysis, device operation, and troubleshooting.

Data Sharing and Collaboration: Farmers, agricultural organizations, and technology providers should collaborate and share data to develop innovative solutions. Open data standards and partnerships can facilitate data sharing and cooperation.

Policy and Regulation: Governments and regulatory bodies should establish clear policies and regulations regarding data privacy, data ownership, and the use of IoT in agriculture. These regulations should balance the need for innovation with environmental and consumer protection.

Sustainability Focus: The next generation of precision farming should prioritize sustainability, including the reduction of environmental impact, the conservation of resources, and the promotion of biodiversity.

Research and Development: Continued research and development in IoT technology and its applications in agriculture are essential. This includes exploring emerging technologies such as AI, blockchain, and edge computing.

Economic Incentives: Governments can provide economic incentives for farmers to adopt IoT technology, such as tax credits for investments in sustainable and innovative agricultural practices.

Market Access: Ensuring that small-scale farmers and farmers in remote areas have access to IoT technology and can benefit from it is crucial. Initiatives to expand market access for these farmers should be developed.

In conclusion, IoT technology has the potential to revolutionize agriculture, making it more efficient, sustainable, and environmentally responsible. Overcoming challenges, embracing upcoming innovations, and preparing for the next generation of precision farming are key steps in harnessing the full potential of IoT in agriculture. As IoT adoption continues to grow, the agriculture industry will be better equipped to meet the food demands of a growing global population while minimizing its environmental impact.

Milton Keynes UK
Ingram Content Group UK Ltd.
UKHW020941221123
433051UK00020B/1023

9 798868 989315